The Table's Story

And Other Observations Instructive to the Christian Journey

Lyndon G. Furst

TEACH Services, Inc.
PUBLISHING
www.TEACHServices.com • (800) 367-1844

World rights reserved. This book or any portion thereof may not be copied or reproduced in any form or manner whatever, except as provided by law, without the written permission of the publisher, except by a reviewer who may quote brief passages in a review.

The author assumes full responsibility for the accuracy of all facts and quotations as cited in this book. The opinions expressed in this book are the author's personal views and interpretations, and do not necessarily reflect those of the publisher.

This book is provided with the understanding that the publisher is not engaged in giving spiritual, legal, medical, or other professional advice. If authoritative advice is needed, the reader should seek the counsel of a competent professional.

Copyright © 2019 Lyndon G. Furst
Copyright © 2019 TEACH Services, Inc.
ISBN-13: 978-1-4796-1017-4 (Paperback)
ISBN-13: 978-1-4796-1018-1 (ePub)
Library of Congress Control Number: 2019902666

Unless otherwise indicated, all Scripture quoted in this book are from the King James Version.

Other scriptures are taken from the Holy Bible, New King James Version Copyright 1979, 1980, 1982, HarperCollins. Used by permission of Thomas Nelson Publishers.

The ESV® Bible (The Holy Bible, English Standard Version®) copyright © 2001 by Crossway Bibles, a publishing ministry of Good News Publishers. The ESV® text has been reproduced in cooperation with and by permission of Good News Publishers. Unauthorized reproduction of this publication is prohibited. All rights reserved.

The Holy Bible New International Version®. (NIV). Copyright © 1973, 1978, 1984 by International Bible Society. All rights reserved.

New Living Translation (NLT). Holy Bible, New Living Translation, copyright © 1996, 2004, 2015 by Tyndale House Foundation. Used by permission of Tyndale House Publishers, Inc., Carol Stream, Illinois 60188. All rights reserved.

Published by

www.TEACHServices.com • (800) 367-1844

Dedication

This book is dedicated to my wife Reva who has stood by my side for nearly 60 years. Through good times and hard times, she has been the one constant in my life. Now, as we age together, she is my principal caregiver. Some of the experiences I have written from my younger years were revealed to her for the first time as she read the early draft of this manuscript. She was not surprised at anything I had written.

In celebration of Mother's Day 2014 at All Nations church in Berrien Springs, Michigan, I was asked to give a brief character sketch of my wife Reva. This can best be done through three short stories.

We were married in 1959 and started our first home in Berrien Springs at 210 College Avenue, right across the street from the Lake Union Conference building. We had three children who have all reached adulthood and have declared their independence. They were good kids, but they were high spirited and had minds of their own, which were not always congruent with their parents' minds.

Our oldest daughter was once involved in a word association game which required her to give a one-word description of various people she knew. The one word she chose for her mother was "helpful."

All of our children have had children of their own who have displayed some of the same characteristics their parents showed in growing up. One day Reva answered the phone to hear our youngest daughter very distraught and crying with big sobs of anguish.

All she had to say was, "Oh, mom, I am so sorry! Can you ever forgive me! I am so sorry!" Reva was puzzled as to what brought on this spell. Then our daughter confessed to her mother that she had been so mean to her and that now she was experiencing the same behavior on the part of her own daughters. "I only have two children," she sobbed. "Oh, mom," she said with a new level of respect for her mother's child raising skills, "how did you ever do it with three of us?"

Reva and I had a casual acquaintance for a few years before we began to get romantically involved. Strict rules on the campus of Emmanuel Missionary College did not allow much time for us to be together. But, the time we did have was very precious to me. At one point in our friendship, my parents came and spent the weekend visiting campus. It was a good time for them to get acquainted with my girlfriend Reva. After a couple of days getting to know her, my father took me aside to give me some counsel, which he had always done quite freely. He mentioned Reva and, looking me sternly in the eye, said, "Son, do not let this one get away!"

The wise man asked: Who can find a virtuous woman? I have found a virtuous woman, and her name is Reva.

Table of Contents

(Dates indicate when the blog was published in the bulletin of the All Nations Seventh-day Adventist church.)

Foreword . . . . *ix*
Introduction to the Spirit of All Nations . . . . *xii*

Part I: The Spirit of All Nations Church

Struggling with a Multicultural Congregation 17
Big Argument in the Church *(Oct. 31, 2015)* 19
At What Table Do You Sit? *(Mar. 26, 2016)* 21
Embarrassed by the Bag Lady *(Apr. 9, 2016)* 23
When You Work Together *(Apr. 30, 2016)* 25
The Table's Story *(Jan. 23, 2016)* 26
He is Really Not so Bad *(Mar. 4, 2017)* 28
We Have Got to Stick Together *(Feb. 11, 2017)* 29
The Faithful Deacon 31
Lessons from the Life of Shamgar *(Jan. 28, 2015)* 33

Part II: Christian Witness

Evangelist on a Harley Davidson 37
A Cup of Coffee and a Piece of Pie 39
What Do You Do for a Living? *(Sept. 26, 2015)* 41

Be Like a Tree *(Oct. 3, 2015)* 42

Please, Lord, Stop Blessing Us! *(Jan. 28, 2017)* 43

Fervent Prayer 45

Born of the Water. 47

We Take Care of You People 49

Even If It Means Your Job? 50

Part III: Thinking of Others

Why Grandpa Cried 55

An Unusual Kindness *(Apr. 1, 2017)* 57

A Most Memorable Christmas 59

Put in a Little More. 61

Part IV: Struggles on the Journey

I Know Because I Know *(Jan. 21, 2017)* 65

The Wicked Flee *(Feb. 18, 2017)* 67

Throw You in a Snow Bank 69

Sin Doth Abound. 71

The Folly of the Fool 73

The Tough Guy was Not so Tough. 75

Johnny and the Chocolate Pudding 77

Lean Not on Your Own Understanding *(Jan. 14, 2017)* 79

Just Wanted to Get Your Attention 80

He Purposed in His Heart *(May 6, 2017)* 82

Water, Cool, Clear Water 84
Put on the Whole Armor. 85

Part V: The Blessed Hope

A Drink of Cold Water. 89
"We Have This Hope"—Part One *(Jan. 9, 2016)*. 91
"We Have This Hope"—Part Two *(Jan. 16, 2016)* 92
Oh, the Dumb Dog! 93
Quite the Surprise *(Apr. 29, 2017)*. 94
Time to Wake Up! 96
The Heavens Declare 97

Part VI: Other Observations

I Do Not Know Why I Stopped *(Apr. 22, 2017)*. 101
Why are You Looking at that Field? 103
I Can Sure Tell That You Are Brothers. 105
Earthy Words. 107
A Father's Counsel to a Wayward Son 109
You Have to Decide 111
When the Answer Is "No" 113
Why the Baby Cried 115
Which the Wind Drives Away 117
Seeking Whom He May Devour. 118
Her Firstborn Son 120

Foreword

When I first became lead pastor of the All Nations Seventh-day Adventist church in Berrien Springs, Michigan, there were days when I would feel pressured by the limited time I had to fulfill all my responsibilities as seminary professor and part-time (really full time) pastor. The straw that would break the camel's back was the blog I had to write for inclusion in the weekly church bulletin. This expectation was especially frustrating when I really wanted to spend more time preparing my sermons.

Then I had a bright idea, one I wish I had thought of earlier. Why not ask long-time member of the congregation, Dr. Lyndon Furst, to write some of these blogs. He writes a column for each issue of *The Journal Era*, the weekly newspaper in Berrien Springs, Michigan. He has a personal and refreshing way of writing stories and personal experiences that I and numerous others greatly enjoy. So, I asked him, and he accepted.

The personal stories that he shared for the blog were sometimes amusing, but always spiritually-focused lessons of life. Jerry, as we call him, took the church on an interesting journey with these stories. We felt like we were right there with him as he related his personal experiences. Readers gained snippets of wisdom in ways that were often humorous yet spiritually engaging. These stories, first written for the All Nations church form the basis for this new devotional book.

After decades of service as a Christian educator, church leader, author, husband, and friend, Jerry has a large reservoir of experiences to draw from for the stories he tells and the fresh devotional journey he will take you on.

Dr. Errol McLean

---

*In addition to his ministry at All Nations Church, Dr. Errol McLean is Associate Director of the North American Division Evangelism Institute. He holds the academic rank of Associate Professor in the Seventh-day Adventist Theological Seminary at Andrews University. Since the time this book was written, Dr. McLean has relinquished the pulpit at All Nations and has returned to his full-time assignment at the Seminary and North American Division.

All Nations Seventh-day Adventist Church in Berrien Springs, Michigan.

Introduction to the Spirit of All Nations

The All Nations Seventh-day Adventist church was founded in 1979 to provide a unique worship experience based on the biblical teachings of intentional inclusion of diverse races, cultures, ethnicities, and ages. It created an environment in which people are affirmed, respected, and celebrated in their differences without allowing those differences to become barriers against the successful implementation of its message. Our identity was defined by our Lord's teaching on unity in diversity in Christ. Its structure was designed to reflect the biblical principle of allowing everyone to have equal access to the privileges and responsibility of service in advancing the mission of the church. Thus, shared leadership is the operative management style.

There was a particular focus on inclusive ministry of compassion through the utilization of the spiritual gifts of the members in identifying and reaching all levels of human concern for social, economic, and political justice, regardless of age, gender, and color. This we tried to accomplish within the context of Christ's ministry of compassion. A significant contribution to our understanding of biblical faith and practice has been the development of a community that seeks to encourage, nurture, and implement fellowship and equality amongst all while respecting culture without being limited by it.

I applaud Dr. Lyndon Furst (known to us as Jerry) for his insights, support, and contributions to the growth and development of All Nations. The insights and contributions that he shared in his many years of unstinted service to All Nations, he now seeks to share with a wider community of believers. Over the years, he has held several leadership positions in the congregation, including but not limited to first elder, resident storyteller, Sabbath School leader, and assistant in the primary Sabbath School. He is well qualified to share his reflections on his experiences as a lifelong member of the Seventh-day Adventist Church.

Dr. Walter B. Douglas

---

*Walter B. Douglas served the Seventh-day Adventist Theological Seminary for thirty-five years while serving for eighteen years as pastor of All Nations Seventh-day Adventist church. As a professor, he served as Chair of the Church History Department. He was the founder and director of the Institute of Diversity and Multiculturalism at Andrews University. He has lectured and conducted seminars and workshops on diversity with intentional inclusion nationally and internationally. In his retirement, in Naples, Florida, he has continued in ministry for thirteen years as the senior pastor of the Golden Gate All Nations Seventh-day Adventist church.

Part I
The Spirit of All Nations Church

Struggling with a Multicultural Congregation

It was an embarrassing moment for me, partly because I just did not know what to do and partly because I did not want to offend the people around me. I was attending a graduation party for one of the members of the All Nations church. All of his cultural friends were present and celebrating just like they would if they were in their home country. I was totally unfamiliar with the markers of their culture. The pastor was out of town, and I, as first elder of the church, was the guest of honor at the celebration.

I was very surprised when they started their ritual with a shout, and one of the teenage girls came running into the room and presented a gift to me. She was followed by another teen who presented me with several dollar bills. I turned to the elder from this ethnic community and said, "I cannot accept these gifts! I should be giving a gift to the graduate." He looked at me with pleading eyes and said, "This is our culture. This is the way we do things at home. Please respect our culture." I reluctantly agreed to do so.

The teens kept bringing gifts to the other elder and me. These included money, a bolt of cloth, and, finally, a case of vegetarian food. I was uneasy with all of the things piling up in front of me,

> "I cannot accept these gifts! I should be giving a gift to the graduate."

but, in the spirit of All Nations, I knew I should respect the cultural traditions of the other members of the congregation.

I had always considered myself to be open-minded toward people from other countries and cultures. However, this experience proved to be a real test of my liberal attitude. The event was an indication to me of the challenges I would face as a member of a multicultural congregation. When one becomes committed to the idea of intentional inclusion of people from all strata of humankind and from diverse cultures, the Holy Spirit can work miracles and overcome the barriers that individuals build up against social and cultural diversity. "All the nations you have made will come and worship before you, Lord; they will bring glory to your name" (Psalm 86:9, NIV).

Big Argument in the Church

There was a big argument in the church. Emotions were flowing at a fevered pitch. The two sides in the dispute were quite far apart on the issue in question. There were strong opinions and strong personalities to give voice to both sides. It looked like compromise on the issue would be impossible to achieve. The arguing raged for a time, but, finally, the participants declared an uneasy truce and accepted a compromise position. Unity was once again restored in the church. The written minutes simply indicated, "There had been much disputing." Nonetheless, one of the participants would later describe the church members as being assembled with one accord. (Read the story in Acts 15.)

How could a church group engage in "much disputing" and yet be described as "being of one accord?" Possibly they found a way to argue their own opinions with a great deal of vigor and, having made their point, were willing to let other members prevail in the dispute.

Several years ago, the All Nations church faced a similar situation. There was a great deal of dissension in the congregation regarding the proper posture one should assume at the time of the morning prayer during the worship hour. Some members thought they should stand in the presence of the Lord, while others felt compelled to kneel. There was much contention and argument. It appeared that the church was dividing along ethnic lines on this issue. Finally, it was put to rest when the congregation reached agreement that members should choose for themselves the posture they would assume during the prayer and accept the decision of the other members who chose a different position.

The members of All Nations come from many different countries and from different cultures within those countries. It is sometimes difficult to find unity when the cultural rules of behavior seem to clash. Our response has been to seek accommodation for cultural variations and maintain sensitivity towards those who are different. Sometimes things will be done that are at odds with our own cultural rules.

This response works because no one culture is allowed to dominate the congregation. Yet, within the parameters of biblical principle, each member can feel safe in maintaining their own cultural practices. Thus, we seek to maintain unity through the acceptance of diversity of culture in church life. Paul gives good counsel to the church members at Rome: "*Be* kindly affectioned one to another with brotherly love; in honour preferring one another" (Rom. 12:10).

At What Table Do You Sit?

Some years ago, the Chair of the Kitchen Committee at All Nations decided to make the potluck meals on Sabbath more dignified by designating a "head table." There, the kitchen crew served the pastor and any visiting dignitaries as well as other prominent leaders of All Nations. The table was set with silverware and fine china. Those sitting at the head table escaped the indignity of standing in line for their food.

All went well until one Sabbath the presiding elder refused to sit at the head table. He strongly opposed the very existence of a head table because it violates the notion of equality of all members, which is a basic principle upon which All Nations was founded. We avoid language that "differentiates between individuals on the basis of social class and status." For example, communications from All Nations do not contain honorific titles.

> All went well until one Sabbath the presiding elder refused to sit at the head table.

The early Christian church experienced similar tensions to All Nations. The Jewish members felt superior to those who had Gentile origins. The situation deteriorated to the point that Peter would no longer sit with Gentiles at mealtime when prominent Jewish members came to visit. Paul saw the hypocrisy and confronted Peter to his face. (See Galatians 2.)

Maintaining a spirit of equality among the entire membership of All Nations requires eternal vigilance. A head table is certainly not within the spirit of the All Nations structure. We can best spread the gospel by maintaining unity in the pursuit of equality. "But, if you show favoritism, you sin and are convicted by the law as lawbreakers" (James 2:9, NIV).

Embarrassed by the Bag Lady

She was not a pretty sight. She stood there in the doorway with disheveled clothes, unkempt hair flying every which direction, and body odor quickly filling all the air pockets in my office. I was principal of an Adventist boarding school. It was camp meeting time, and members from around the state occupied the campus. I had many requests from people who wanted to visit the classrooms. Now, this woman wanted me to give her a personal guided tour.

I could not find a good excuse to deny her request. So I escorted her through the building to visit each of the classrooms. I was embarrassed to be seen with a person who looked like a bag lady from the big city. Several church dignitaries and wealthy members (potential donors) were on campus. What would they think of me in the presence of such a character?

In reflection sometime later, I remembered James 2:9, "If you show partiality you commit sin." The All Nations church is guided by the principles of equality of believers and intentional inclusiveness. In contrast to my feelings towards the "bag lady," we find no room for partiality on the basis of race, gender, age, social class, education, or capability. "Humble yourselves in the sight of the Lord, and He will lift you up" (James 4:10, NKJV).

24 ❳ *The Table's Story*

When You Work Together

Some years ago, my two granddaughters from Minnesota came to visit. One morning I suggested to Chloe, the oldest, that we put a puzzle together. It soon became apparent that the puzzle was a bit too hard for her. To be helpful, I suggested that we pick out all the border pieces first and then get all those with similar colors together. She caught on quite quickly for a five-year-old, I thought.

Once we got organized, I discovered the puzzle was not too difficult for her. She was much better than I at finding pieces that matched. My trifocals were no match for her sharp young eyes. She noticed the details, while to me it was all just a blur of color. Soon the picture was complete.

I remarked on how nice the puzzle looked when all put together. My energetic five-year-old with the sharp eyes summed up our efforts with a profound statement. "It is much easier when you work together, Grandpa," she said. And so it was that the two of us accomplished much more together then if we had worked separately. I provided the strategy, and she took care of the details.

Chloe learned this lesson well. She insisted on helping make lunch because it is much easier when we work together. Even when it came time to do the dishes, she wanted to help, because working together makes that unpleasant task much easier. When we work together, we can accomplish much more than if we work separately. "Two *are* better than one" (Eccl. 4:9, NKJV).

The Table's Story

We have a small wooden table in our house that captivates the attention of everyone who visits us. It is nothing but a piece of driftwood that I made into a table. The table has a story to tell.

I, with several friends, found this piece of wood thrashing in the surf on the beach in northern California. We suspected that it was not just an ordinary piece of driftwood, so we plunged into the surf and, with much effort, rolled it onto a four-wheel-drive pickup.

A member of our congregation whose hobby was making useful items from driftwood identified the shapeless clump as a burl (an irregular growth) from a Pepperwood tree. The violent rainstorms of the previous winter caused a flood-swollen river to deposit the burl in the Pacific Ocean.

Our friend knew exactly what to do. "Let it dry for several weeks," he said. "Then I will have my brother, Clarence, saw it into slabs for you." In those days, Clarence, aged 40, was classified as "mentally retarded." Yet, he had one skill that none of us possessed. He could guide a five-foot lance tooth crosscut saw across an irregular clump of wood with great precision. Because this simple man, with only one talent, was willing to use this one skill, I now have a beautiful Pepperwood burl table in my living room.

I am reminded of the parable of the three stewards in which two of the stewards utilized their abilities to increase their master's wealth while the third declined to do so. To those who had been faithful, the master's words were, "'Well *done*, good and faithful servant; you were faithful over a few things, I will make you ruler over many things. Enter into the joy of your lord'" (Matt. 25:21, NKJV).

He is Really Not so Bad

Everybody in the room looked at me in amazement and began to ridicule me for the really stupid suggestion I had just made in our class meeting. All of the popular teachers had been chosen by the upper grades to be their class sponsor, and we were left with no really good choices among the remaining faculty and staff. Then a strange idea popped into my head, and, before I could give it serious thought, I just blurted it out. I suggested that we choose the most disliked member of the faculty as our class sponsor.

Mr. Taft was the farm manager at our boarding school. He was a grumpy old fellow, and I had had a major confrontation with him early in the school year. So, almost as a joke, I suggested we choose him for our faculty sponsor. Then, I mentioned that part of Mr. Taft's responsibility was purchasing food for the cafeteria. He could get ice cream and other goodies at wholesale prices for our class parties. Suddenly my suggestion didn't look so stupid.

The principal was surprised at our choosing Mr. Taft to be our class sponsor. Mr. Taft could hardly believe it himself. In the twenty-five years he had worked in Adventist boarding schools, he had never been chosen to be a class sponsor. He invited us to his home, individually and as a whole class. He did indeed get ice cream for our parties at low cost. We found that what we had seen as a grumpy old man wasn't so bad after all. As I have thought about Mr. Taft over the years, I have come to realize how easy it is to misjudge people by their outward appearance and seemingly strange behaviors. "For man looks at the outward appearance, but the Lord looks at the heart" (1 Sam. 16:7, NKJV).

We Have Got to Stick Together

It was a dark and stormy night, and I was lost. Oh, I knew that I was on a big lake in the Boundary Waters of Northern Minnesota, but I was not quite certain of my exact location on that lake. There were four of us in two canoes, and we were heading home after several days of canoeing. My long-time friend and partner, Ned, paddled on the left side of the canoe while I preferred the right. In the other canoe, Gayle, who was a real outdoorsman and leader of our little group, sat in the back while Bob sat up front. Ned and I paddled with slow even strokes, while the other two went at it fast and furious. We had such different styles.

Gayle suddenly decided that he needed to get home a day earlier than our original plan. Putting our best effort into it, we could arrive at our parked vehicle by midnight. I had the map and was appointed navigator. The sun set and the storm clouds blotted out the starry sky. Gayle gave strict instructions, "We have got to stick together." It was hard going, navigating in the dark. I made the fateful decision to take a shortcut around the large island that blocked our way and soon became disoriented. Fortunately, some campers on the island enjoying their campfire pointed us in the right direction.

A light drizzling rain and the rolling thunder in the far distance motivated Ned and me to become fast paddlers. About 100 yards up a little stream we found the trailhead for the portage over a steep hill to the next lake. It was slippery and treacherous carrying our canoes, especially in the dark. We had several near accidents but eventually arrived at our destination. Following Gayle's firm instruction, "We have got to stick together," got us safely through that dark and stormy night.

Our spiritual journey is much safer when we stick together in the church, helping each other. No matter what our differences, we have got to stick together. "Not forsaking the assembling of ourselves together, as *is* the manner of some, but exhorting *one another*, and so much the more as you see that Day approaching" (Heb. 10:25, NKJV).

The Faithful Deacon

Several years ago, I lived in a Midwestern city of moderate size. The only Seventh-day Adventist church in that part of the state was very conservative. Change came hard to them, yet my wife and I made good friends there. My wife remarked to me one Sabbath, after divine service, that one of the younger members of our congregation (I will call him Brandon) routinely would go around the sanctuary as the members left, and he would pick up any loose papers and other trash that had been left on the floor and between the pews. We discovered that no one had assigned him that task; he just saw that it needed to be done and did it.

> *We discovered that no one had assigned him that task; he just saw that it needed to be done and did it.*

During the year, the head deacon moved, and I was asked to fill in for the rest of the year. We did not have a large group of deacons, so each one had to be on duty at least two Sabbaths each month. When I asked the nominating committee to make Brandon a deacon, there was a negative reaction from both the pastor and one of the longtime members of the congregation. "He is too young for that high position," they told me. "Let him mature a little before he is put into such an office." I responded that Brandon was the most faithful deacon I had. Nonetheless, the members stood fast in their conviction that he was not mature enough for the position.

How refreshing it was to come to All Nations where youth are highly valued and placed in positions of responsibility within the church. I am reminded of instructions given to a young minister in the early church. "Let no one despise your youth, but be an example to the believers in word, in conduct, in love, in spirit, in faith, in purity" (1 Tim. 4:12, NKJV).

Lessons from the Life of Shamgar

I am interested in little-known characters in history that had a significant impact on their particular corner of the world. The accomplishment of one such person is found in a single verse in Judges 3. "And after him was Shamgar the son of Anath, which slew of the Philistines six hundred men with an ox goad: and he also delivered Israel" (Judges 3:31). It might be surprising, but there are things we can learn from this one short verse.

At the time Shamgar lived, God directed the Israelites to possess the land He had designated for them. That operation was not going well. However, Shamgar had visions of larger things than just the small part of the land they had occupied to that point. Therefore, he proceeded to do the work that needed to be done, and he did it without a great deal of publicity.

Shamgar was not afraid to confront superior numbers. He did so without special training or even the proper instruments of war. In obeying God's command to drive out the inhabitants of the Promised Land, he used the talents and tools he already had.

What an excellent example for the members of All Nations. We can apply those same characteristics to our own situation here in Berrien Springs as we obey God's command to preach the gospel in this community.

While this story was originally written for All Nations Church, it provides good counsel for all believers who wish to participate in the gospel commission.

Part II
Christian Witness

Evangelist on a Harley Davidson

I first met Gary at a class reunion at the second of the three boarding academies that I was privileged to attend. He had attended in his freshman and senior years while I had attended in my sophomore and junior years. At the reunion, I was anxious to get better acquainted with Gary and his wife Karen. Eventually they told me the story of their chosen mission to advance the gospel. They both love to ride motorcycles and joined a biker's club, the Christian Motorcycle Association (CMA). They decided not just to ride with their club but to attend other biker rallies where there were no Christians. They would simply show up at a rally and look for ways to be helpful. They tried to attend the same events every year so they could get personally acquainted with people. For twenty years they have attended such biker events as "Woody's Pig Roast," where they have helped with the feeding of the group (as many as 600) and the clean up of the mess when it was over. Even though they do not eat the food they serve, they are as helpful as possible to see that mealtime goes smoothly.

Gary and Karen silently witness by wearing their own biker's leather vest with the logo of a cross, praying hands, and a Bible. Without initiating a religious discussion, they simply lend a helping hand and a listening ear wherever they go. Traveling as many as 6,000 miles a year, they find that motorcycles attract a certain crowd of people and make it easy to conduct evangelism on a personal scale. Resistance to the message of the gospel seems to melt away when a biker approaches them with curiosity about Christianity or for help with personal issues. With the guidance of the Holy Spirit, they are able to minister to the spiritual needs of this unique group where other evangelistic approaches have not penetrated.

In Jesus' day, He was criticized by religious leaders for socializing with a rough crowd. When Jesus heard of it, he said to them, "They that are whole need not a physician; but they that are sick. I came not to call the righteous, but sinners to repentance" (Luke 5:31, 32).

A Cup of Coffee and a Piece of Pie

When my father retired after thirty years in the ministry, he was still full of energy, so he continued to serve the church by pastoring two small congregations that were several miles apart. During the week, he frequently had to travel between the two churches to give Bible studies, conduct prayer meetings, or visit the members. Dad discovered a small restaurant located on the highway he traveled that advertised homemade pie. Dad liked to stop there on weekdays to get a piece of pie. That is when I discovered that he liked to drink coffee with his pie.

> Dad discovered a small restaurant located on the highway he traveled that advertised homemade pie.

My father was a gregarious sort and easily struck up a conversation with the waitress who served him. He usually stopped there during a time when there were not many customers. The waitress was not so busy and enjoyed conversing with Dad about a variety of subjects. It was not long before Dad turned the conversation to religion and the relationship one has with the Creator God. The waitress seemed interested, so Dad, always alert to the opportunity for personal evangelism, suggested that she might be interested in a more formal study of the Bible. She readily agreed.

She had been talking to her family about the conversations she had with the retired minister and, when she mentioned the upcoming Bible studies at her home, her husband expressed interest in being included. The waitress and her parents were there when Dad arrived. Soon, her husband's parents showed up to take part in the Bible studies. They were fascinated with the discovery of Adventist beliefs and soon accepted the teachings of the Bible that had been presented to them.

Because of Dad's desire for a cup of coffee and piece of pie, six people were baptized into the little country church where he pastored. My father's knack for seizing any opportunity to teach the gospel of Jesus was a gift of the Holy Spirit. He employed that gift very well.

"Now concerning spiritual *gifts*, brethren, I would not have you ignorant. But the manifestation of the Spirit is given to every man to profit withal" (1 Cor. 12:1, 7).

What Do You Do for a Living?

Several years ago, I agreed to a series of Bible studies with a Jehovah's Witness. Every week he came to my home to study the Bible with me. He always brought a companion with him from their congregation.

I am by nature a curious person. So I asked one of the men that my Witness friend brought with him what he did for a living. His response was, "I give Bible studies."

Thinking he misunderstood my question, I rephrased it. "What kind of job do you have?"

"My job is giving Bible studies," was his response.

Frustrated that he was playing word tricks with me I tried again. "What kind of work do you do?" He came right back with, "My work is to give Bible studies."

I was tired of the game, so I said, "Look, you cannot pay your bills giving Bible studies. You must have some way of earning money."

His response was startling. "Oh, money," he said. "I sell stocks and bonds for money, but for a living, I give Bible studies."

There was a time when the Adventist people took the gospel commission as their marching orders. The last words of Jesus to His disciples as He was leaving this world are instructive. "But ye shall receive power, after that the Holy Ghost is come upon you: and ye shall be witnesses unto me both in Jerusalem, and in all Judaea, and in Samaria, and unto the uttermost part of the earth" (Acts 1:8).

Be Like a Tree

I was quite young when my family left our home place in Minnesota and eventually moved to the state of Wyoming. The barren high plains provided quite a contrast with the verdant greenery of our home state. As we headed west out of Cheyenne, the entire family began to question the wisdom of this move. Cheyenne was not much more than a village with hardly any greenery. Laramie, the next town, was not much better.

No matter how desolate the landscape, there was no turning back, as this was my father's first assignment after graduating from Union College with a degree in religion. We had grown weary of seeing nothing but sagebrush and sand, which dominated the scenery. Then we noticed a thin ribbon of green far in the distance. It seemed to stretch all across the horizon.

As we continued on, we discovered the North Platte River with trees growing all along its banks. We soon learned that in Wyoming, whenever you see green things growing, it is a sign that water is nearby. Psalm 1 describes the righteous as being "like a tree planted by the rivers of water." The question now comes: how do others view me? Is my example a sign that the Water of Life is nearby?

Please, Lord, Stop Blessing Us!

At the beginning of our marriage, my wife, Reva, and I committed ourselves to pay tithe (ten percent of our income). We both worked for the college at student wages, and we consistently tithed our meager income every month. Then the pastor presented a new plan proposed by the leaders of the church, that, in addition to the tithe, members should be encouraged to pay an additional two percent of income for the combined budget. I expressed my doubt that we could afford to pay that much more. My wife had more faith than I did and convinced me we should follow the plan.

In planning for the future, we rented a parcel of land behind what is now the Adventist Book Center and planted a big garden. It was hard work preparing the soil with hand tools. It was also hard work weeding and cultivating the rows of vegetables as they began to grow. The Lord blessed us by sending sunshine and rain to replenish the soil.

We had a productive garden, especially the green string beans. The Lord blessed us with beans, and He blessed us with more beans, and He continued to bless us with so many beans that I wanted to shout, "Please, Lord, stop blessing us!" We had more produce from the garden than we could possibly eat, so we gave the surplus to other married students who were in the same economic straits that we were in. I never thought I would see the time when God would pour out more blessings than I could receive. But that's exactly what happened. "'Test me in this,' says the LORD Almighty, 'and see if I will not throw open the floodgates of heaven and pour out so much blessing that there will not be room enough to store it'" (Mal. 3:10, NIV).

Fervent Prayer

Several years ago, I was elected to the board of the public school district in our community. One of the members on the board was an engineer who had a negative disposition. He was against almost everything that any of the other board members supported. He was especially critical of the superintendent as well as of the professional staff that was employed by the school district. I periodically clashed with him in board meetings because we had distinctly different views on the operation of the schools.

One evening, just prior to the board meeting, the superintendent asked us to tour the lower elementary school building so we could view first-hand some needs of the physical plant. When we finished our tour of the building, we walked together about 100 yards to the board meeting. I happened to be walking with the negative board member. He mentioned an item on the agenda regarding the purchase of computers for one of the classrooms. He was upset by the proposal from the superintendent. "It is a waste of money," he said, with more than a little anger in his voice. "I plan to give the superintendent a hard time about this."

I really did not have energy for such a public confrontation and gave a quick prayer for wisdom to deal with the issue. I knew that some of the other board members were believers in the power of prayer. We were all from different faith communities—Adventist, Catholic, Pentecostal, Lutheran, and Methodist. I quietly invited those I knew to be practicing Christians to join me in another room before the board meeting.

I briefly explained what the negative board member had told me and suggested that, since we were all "believers," we should pray that God would intervene and protect us from a disruptive meeting. When the item in question was presented, it was voted with very little discussion. The negative board member said not a word as we proceeded with the agenda. Certainly, the angels had been sent to intervene in answer to our prayer. "The prayer of a righteous man is powerful and effective" (James 5:16, NIV).

Born of the Water

It was a warm sunny day on that Sabbath afternoon in southern Wyoming. Several members of the Seventh-day Adventist church in the rural community had gathered on the banks of Snake River just on the edge of the little town of Dixon (current population 97). The river is just a mountain stream with smooth rounded rocks for the riverbed. The occasion was a baptism conducted by my father who was the pastor of the Adventist church. A couple of adults and two or three other young people like me were also candidates for baptism. I was to be the first person my father baptized in his ministry.

I was quite young for making such a momentous decision, but I felt ready for baptism and the responsibility of church membership. I had discussed baptism with my father several times. Eventually, he agreed with my childish desires, but, he insisted that I be prepared by studying the doctrines of the church. He had a pamphlet that provided a step-by-step study of the Bible from an Adventist perspective. It was not written for children, but I had no trouble getting through it because I had heard most of it from Dad's preaching.

The baptism was held on the property of one of our church members who made his river access available for the event. I watched as my father carefully walked to the middle of the stream. The rocky bed was very slippery, and I had to step gingerly as I approached deep water. The little company of believers was singing the refrain to the hymn, "The Cleansing Stream." "The cleansing stream, I see, I see! I plunge, and, oh it cleanseth me!" Then

Dad lowered me into the swift-flowing stream. I expected that my life would be changed the moment I was taken up out of the water. How disappointed I was when I did not see a big patch of my sins floating down the river.

> Later, one of the church members asked, "How do you feel now that you are baptized?"

Later, one of the church members asked, "How do you feel now that you are baptized?" I really did not feel anything different. I had been born of the water but not yet of the Spirit. I later came to realize that, for me, this was an important first step in a long journey with the Lord. "Unless one is born of water and the Spirit, he cannot enter the kingdom of God" (John 3:5, NKJV).

We Take Care of You People

Many years ago, I attended a university on the West Coast where I eventually received my advanced graduate degree. It was my first experience outside of the Seventh-day Adventist higher education system. One thing I wanted to do before graduating was to join Phi Delta Kappa, the professional fraternity for leaders in education. To learn all the steps I needed to take to join this prestigious organization, I went to the orientation session. The fraternity had a long-standing tradition that new members had to go through an induction ceremony prior to being admitted. It was scheduled for Friday night. I approached the leader and mentioned that I could not attend on that date. "Oh," he said. "There is another chapter of the fraternity at a nearby university, and you can go there to be inducted." Unfortunately, their ceremony was also on Friday night.

When he quizzed me as to why every Friday night seemed to be a conflict in schedule, I said, "Well, I am a Seventh-day Adventist and …" Before I could complete the sentence, he interrupted me and said, "Oh, we take care of you people." Then he explained to me that they had a practice session for the ritual prior to the time of the event. He said, "We will be able to get the practice session done in time for you to get home and have sundown worship with your family."

I never did find out how he knew so much about Seventh-day Adventist tradition, but somebody must have prepared the way by their example. God promised the ancient Israelites, "Behold, I send an Angel before you to keep you in the way and to bring you into the place which I have prepared" (Exod. 23:20, NKJV).

Even If It Means Your Job?

I first met Dan at the third Seventh-day Adventist boarding academy I attended during my high school years. As first-year seniors, we had a mutual interest in helping each other adjust to the academy environment. In college, we shared a dormitory room for a couple of years. We both got married the same summer and lived not far apart as we continued our higher education. Eventually, we both ran short of finances and dropped out of school. There were no grants, scholarships, or student loans in those days. We found work in an automobile factory twenty miles from where we lived.

Dan was assigned to the pickup division where he worked as a welder. Sales of pickup trucks were very good at the time. My assignment seemed a bit more exotic. I was on a three-person team welding several small parts together for the ventilation system on the sports car.

One day the superintendent in Dan's department announced to all the employees, "We are going on six days starting next week. Everyone will be here on Saturday for their usual work assignment. No exceptions!"

My friend Dan gulped at the foreman's firm statement. He had long ago committed himself to keeping the Sabbath holy as God's commandment requires. He told the foreman, "I am a Seventh-day Adventist and do not work on Saturdays. That is my Sabbath." The foreman did not look impressed and said, "Well, I made it clear that there will be no exceptions." Dan quietly responded that he understood the announcement, but he would not be at work on Saturday.

"Would you still feel that way if it meant your job?" the foreman retorted. Dan quickly answered, "Yes, even if it means my job." Just as he started to walk away, the foreman looked at Dan and said, "That is the right answer. Don't worry about it, we will work something out." The foreman was aware of the commitment that Adventists had made to God's Sabbath, and he was simply testing the strength of Dan's resolve. "Six days you shall labor and do all your work, but the seventh day is a sabbath to the LORD your God. On it you shall not do any work" (Exod. 20:9, 10, NIV).

Part III
Thinking of Others

Why Grandpa Cried

I was always very fond of my grandfather. When I grew up and had a family of my own, I wanted my children to become acquainted with my grandparents. We tried to visit them on summer vacations whenever possible. One summer, my father asked me to help repair the roof on a part of Grandpa's old house. Neither my grandfather nor my father was in physical condition to be on a ladder doing roofing, so the major part of the task fell to me. I am not very handy, but I gave it my best effort.

Grandparents Nelson (Nick) and Ellen Davis.

I finally got all the old shingles removed from that steep roof, but, as darkness approached, I realized we could never get the roof done on that day. I just prayed that it would not rain that night. Unfortunately, my pleas with the Courts Above were not heard with favor, and it did rain. My grandparents were rudely awakened from their sleep by water dripping on their bed. They spent most of the night huddled on the couch in the living room downstairs.

The next day when I surveyed the mess caused by the leaky roof, I apologized profusely to my grandparents. My pleas for forgiveness were interrupted when my grandfather began to cry. Those great sobs tore at my heart. Grandpa saw my anguish, and he reassured me it was not the leaky roof that brought his outpouring of tenderness but, rather, his sorrow at news of floods in the nearby state. "I feel so sorry for those poor people in South Dakota," he said. "So many of them have lost their homes. I'm just so thankful to have a home even if the roof did leak." So, that is why Grandpa cried, not for his own loss but for the greater loss of others. He was content to have a home—even one with a defective roof. "Now, godliness with contentment is great gain" (1 Tim. 6:6, NKJV).

An Unusual Kindness

As a teenager, I did a lot of foolish things—none of which I will describe in detail. However, I did have some experiences that made a lasting impression on me. In one instance, I was hitchhiking in Western Montana with my friend Larry. We were both fifteen years old, and we thought we were quite wise in matters of this world.

On a cold October night, we found ourselves stranded alongside the railroad tracks several miles from the city of Butte. We had hopped a freight train when we could not get a ride on the highway. The steam engine stopped to connect with some additional train cars on a siding and the car we were in was disconnected.

We didn't really know exactly where we were, but we realized it was a long way from Butte. We saw some lights in the distance and decided to see if there were someplace we could get in out of the cold. It was a saloon, open late at night. We told the bartender our predicament, and he advised us to stay there until workers on the late shift at the nearby chemical plant stopped by on their way home. Soon, several men came in to slake their thirst and get a snack. I could see the bartender talking to them and pointing at us. The next thing I knew, one of the men came over to us and told us he would take us to town.

Our new friend had just moved from one apartment to another and still had a bed in the old apartment. He let us stay there for the night. Then, when morning came, he took us to his house where his wife fed us a good breakfast. He gave each of us some money and took us out to the edge of town so we could catch a ride to our destination. I will never forget the kindness of that stranger to two foolish teenagers who hopped a freight train in Western Montana. "Whatever you did for one of the least of these brothers of mine, you did for me" (Matt. 25:40, NIV).

A Most Memorable Christmas

When I was quite young, my parents decided to move to Lincoln, Nebraska, so my father could pursue the ministerial course at Union College. There were no loans or grants in those days, so Dad had to work as much as he could to pay his tuition and support a family. To make the move, we had an auction and sold most of our possessions. During his last year in college, we faced a very bleak Christmas. Dad confided in me that we did not have any money for a tree and decorations or even for gifts for us kids. Even at a young age, I understood what living on the edge of poverty meant, so I was ready before Dad had his little talk with me.

> Soon after we had cleared the table from supper and settled in our living room for the evening, we heard a loud knock at the door.

Then, suddenly, the plans changed. After supper on Christmas Eve, Dad took me aside and told me that there would be a Christmas after all. His major professor, the Chair of the History Department, was going to come and play Santa Claus at our home that evening. But he wanted it to be a surprise for my little brother, Bob. Soon after we had cleared the table from supper and settled in our living room for the evening, we heard a loud knock at the door. Dad sent me with Bob to answer the door. There was the learned professor all dressed up in a red Santa suit with a bag of toys over his shoulder loudly proclaiming, "Ho, ho, ho! Merry Christmas!" Bob was frightened at the sight and ran to the safety of our mother's arms.

Then Santa began distributing the toys, which far exceeded my wildest anticipation. I recognized that they were not brand-new and that some showed signs of much wear. Yet, the unexpected thoughtfulness of my father's college history professor made for a most memorable Christmas. From my perspective, simple acts of kindness make life in this harsh world tolerable and provide pleasant memories for many years to come. That is the true spirit of Christmas. "Whoever is generous to the poor lends to the Lord, and he will repay him for his deed" (Prov. 19:17, ESV).

Put in a Little More

I have very fond childhood memories of my grandfather. He was the youngest son in a family with eighteen children, and he inherited the least productive half of his father's homestead in west central Minnesota. Through hard work and frugal living, he pulled a reasonably comfortable living from that small farm. Just before the Great Depression, he purchased a brand-new Model A Ford touring car, which was the talk of that rural community in those days.

My father left farming when I was quite young, but we frequently returned to help Grandpa during summer vacation. He milked a few cows by hand and sold the cream. He supplemented that meager income with a large garden. He peddled the produce to the resort people around the lakes nearby. My cousin and I would ride on the running boards of the Model A as Grandpa drove from cabin to cabin, helping him sell his produce.

One summer day early in the morning as we were harvesting vegetable produce to be sold later that day, I saw Grandpa carefully weighing a sack of vegetables on his mechanical scale. Each sack contained two pounds. I observed him weighing on his scales trying to get the exact amount. He saw me watching and told me that, when he got exactly two pounds in the sack, he always put in another handful, just to give his customers more than what they paid for.

That made a tremendous impression on me in my pre-teen years. I have tried to follow Grandpa's example by giving more than what I am paid for. In that spirit, I have added an extra devotional to this little book, which originally was planned for one story each week for a year. I hope you enjoyed the book and the little more that I have put in it. "He that hath a bountiful eye shall be blessed" (Prov. 22:9).

Grandpa Nelson (Nick) Davis.

Part IV

Struggles on the Journey

I Know Because I Know

It was the summer of my discontent. I was struggling with matters of faith while working on an advanced degree at a university in central California. A professor of sociology was hostile towards organized religion—especially Christianity. He was quite effective in challenging the basis of my belief system. A mountain of evidence supports religion as merely the "opiate of the masses," he claimed.

I could not make a rational argument, based on solid evidence, in support of my religion. Faith and emotion provided the sole foundation for my chosen belief system. I was adopted into a Seventh-day Adventist family and grew up in the church. Now, for the first time, I was confronted with doubt. It was going to be a long hot summer as I grappled with this new experience.

One day, as I walked across campus, an old song came to mind. It brought back memories of the second Adventist boarding school I attended. The dean of boys decided that our repertoire of worship music needed to be expanded, so he taught us several new tunes. Now, some fifteen years later, the melody of one of those songs began playing over and over in my head.

Then the words came to my memory. "I know not how this saving faith to me He did impart, nor how believing in His word wrought peace within my heart." The chorus contained the answer to the question that troubled me. "I know whom I have believed, and am persuaded that he is able to keep that which I have committed unto him against that day" (2 Tim. 1:12).

There are some things, I concluded, that we know only because we know. They are not discovered by rational processes but by faith alone. When I realized that the rules of science are not appropriate to matters of faith, my lifelong faith in God was affirmed.

(A longer version of this story is found in *Avenues to the Heart*, Larry Blackmer, ed. Pacific Press, 2006)

The Wicked Flee

It happened at the second of the three boarding schools I attended during my high school years. This school had the family plan for dining rather than a cafeteria. We usually had assigned seating at each meal, but Friday supper was open seating. One Friday evening I noted that, with the regular food at the table, there was a small dish of tapioca pudding at each place. It was a pleasant surprise because we seldom had dessert of any kind.

I was sitting with my closest friends, and we were in good spirits. We were laughing and joking and having a wonderful time. I realized that we had become far too loud when I felt a gentle tap on my shoulder. I knew without looking that it was Mrs. Alloway, the matron of the dining hall.

> *One Friday evening I noted that, with the regular food at the table, there was a small dish of tapioca pudding at each place.*

Mrs. Alloway was a wonderful lady but very strict about student behavior at mealtime. A student who got out of control would be sent from the dining room without a chance to finish the meal. I panicked because I feared the pudding would be snatched from my grasp as I was expelled from the room. Without pausing to think about it, I grabbed the dish of tapioca and gobbled it down just as fast as I could.

I must have made quite a scene because the whole dining hall was convulsed in laughter. Mrs. Alloway was laughing just as hard as the students. She was not going to discipline me. She just wanted to ask me a question about something. I had a feeling of guilt when there was no need for me to be afraid of the potential consequences. I not only made a fool out of myself in front of all the students, but I didn't really get to savor the pudding. "The wicked flee when no one pursues" (Prov. 28:1, NKJV).

Throw You in a Snow Bank

When I was about ten years old, a retired sheep rancher in southern Wyoming gave us a small dog, a poodle, for a pet. He soon became an integral part of our family although I claimed him as my own. I named him "Teddy." Eventually, I left home to go to boarding school and then to college. Yet, every time I came home my dog Teddy welcomed me with such energy that I knew he had not forgotten me.

Teddy had a very excitable temperament, and the slightest disturbance would set him to barking. One winter we had an unusually big drift of snow around the front porch of our house. As Teddy got excited, one of those frigid days, and was making a big fuss about something, my father grabbed him and took him to the front door, all the way repeating over and over, "I'm going to throw you in the snow bank!"

Dad opened the front door and threw Teddy out into a three-foot bank of snow. It took Teddy quite a bit of effort before he was able to extract himself. Teddy learned his lesson well. After that, whenever he made a fuss, all we had to do was say, "Throw you in a snow bank!" and Teddy would quiet down right away.

Sometimes we go through hard experiences that are needed to help us mature in our Christian life. Yet, we can claim the promise that God will not allow us to be tested above our ability to endure. "But God *is* faithful, who will not suffer you to be tempted above that ye are able; but will with the temptation also make a way to escape, that ye may be able to bear *it*" (1 Cor. 10:13).

To see a short video of Teddy, go to: http://1ref.us/r5

Sin Doth Abound

During my teen years, I was privileged to attend three different Seventh-day Adventist boarding schools. The first academy was located in a western state near a small town. It was in a pleasant rural setting, except for one thing. The railroad tracks ran right near the campus property. My first night there, I learned that a freight train was scheduled to pass by the campus at 4 o'clock in the morning.

In time, I got used to the train coming through. One day one of my classmates had a brilliant idea for some fun. He suggested that we get some fully matured cattails and pull them all apart over the tracks. We wanted to see what would happen when a freight train hit that big mound of cattail fluff.

Plants from the genus *Typha* are known in England as bulrushes, but, in America, we call them cattails. When fully mature, their fruit can be pulled apart easily with many thousands of little seeds in each plant. It was not difficult for us to make a huge mound of cattail fluff across the railroad tracks.

When we woke up in the morning, we could tell the 4 o'clock train had made its run, because there was cattail fluff all over the campus in every building. The fluff had floated down the stairways to my basement dormitory room. It was a hilarious sight, but not so much fun cleaning up the mess afterward.

Our world is somewhat like the academy campus when the freight train hit the big pile of cattail fluff. Sin is everywhere present and contaminates every part of the planet. But we have the promise, that "where sin abounded, grace did much more abound" (Rom. 5:20). Thank God for the gift of grace that is given so freely.

The Folly of the Fool

It happened at the third Adventist boarding school I attended during my high school years. My room was on the third floor where we had very little supervision. One of my classmates confided in me that he had brought a small television set to a friend's house on the edge of campus, and he asked me for help in getting it to his room in the dormitory. This was in the days when TV was just becoming popular, and I quickly agreed to help.

We put the TV set in the kneehole of his desk, draped some of his clothing over the desk, and did the same to a chair placed in front of it. It looked like a normal boy's messy room. The dean turned the lights off at the main switch in his office at 10:30 every night. I, being a monitor, was designated by my classmates to see that the switch for the exit lights was turned on because that was the source of electricity to this one room. We invited only other seniors to join us for television every night.

After graduation, the story of how we fooled the dean in having a TV in the dorm was retold many times. Years later, the dean was visiting in the area where I lived, so some of my former classmates who lived nearby decided to have a mini class reunion. After our meal, we were reminiscing about the good times at the academy. One of my classmates suggested that we should confess to the dean how we had fooled him in having a television set in a dormitory room. I was chosen as the designated confessor.

When I confessed our deception, the dean remarked, "Oh, yes, it was in that corner room on third floor, in the kneehole of the desk. When you boys were in classes, I watched the baseball games on the television." For twenty-five years, we thought we had gotten away with deceiving the dean, while he knew about it the whole time. We were the real fools in this story. "The wisdom of the prudent *is* to understand his way: but the folly of fools *is* deceit" (Prov. 14:8).

The Tough Guy was Not so Tough

While working on a road construction crew in the Upper Peninsula of Michigan one summer, I became good friends with one of the younger crewmembers, whose name was Jim. He was a tough guy and ran with a tough crowd when he was not at work. He was a heavy drinker and he smoked two packs of cigarettes a day. I discovered that his smoking habit was his real Achilles' heel. One day the foreman told Jim and me that the project superintendent needed somebody to finish up a small part of a job that was left over from another crew. We needed to take our lunch buckets with us because it would take most of the day to finish the project. The superintendent picked us up in mid-morning and took us to the remote site.

> I noticed Jim becoming quite agitated because he always smoked at least one cigarette right after lunch.

As we were working there, Jim let out a sudden cry of apprehension. He had not checked his cigarette supply before he left for work. He had only two cigarettes left in his pack, and he knew that would not get him through the day. By noon the cigarette pack was empty. We ate our lunch sitting beside the road. I noticed Jim becoming quite agitated because he always smoked at least one cigarette right after lunch. I began to tease him. I told him how good a smoke would be right now. I described in detail the pleasures of a cigarette after lunch. Jim begged and pleaded with me to stop taunting him.

I noticed way down the road a truck coming our way. Jim was so desperate for a smoke that he actually ran down and stood in the middle of the road waving his arms so the driver would stop. Without hesitation, Jim asked if he could bum a cigarette off him. The driver laughed and gave him a couple to hold him over until our shift was done. That is how I discovered that the tough guy was not so tough after all. He had become ensnared by tobacco, which placed a heavy weight on him. In thinking about my friend Jim, I remembered a verse in Hebrews: "Let us lay aside every weight, and the sin which so easily ensnares *us*" (Heb. 12:1, NKJV).

Johnny and the Chocolate Pudding

by Bernard J. Furst,
as told to his sons, Lyndon Gerald, Robert James,
and Joseph Nelson Furst

Johnny loved chocolate pudding, especially the kind his mother made from scratch. This was in the days before prepackaged ready-to-eat foods. As Mother stirred the magic potion, its fragrance wafted through the house and was soon strongly attached to the insides of Johnny's nostrils.

Johnny's mother had to do some shopping. She told Johnny that she would be gone for at least an hour, and he was not to eat the pudding that was cooling on the countertop. He went outside to play, but within an hour he had become bored. He went into the house and noticed that bowl of pudding on the countertop. As he looked at it, he remembered his promise to his mother.

Twice more he came in from the backyard, but mother was still not home. Each time he noticed the bowl of pudding. But he was an obedient boy, so he did not take any. By the third time that he came back into the house, he was getting quite hungry, and mother still was not home from her shopping trip. As Johnny stared hungrily at that bowl of chocolate pudding, he saw something he had never noticed before.

When pudding cools, it shrinks, and in the process, it leaves a little ribbon of dry pudding around the bowl. Mother did not say anything about not eating the dried ribbon around the inside of the bowl. Using a small spoon, Johnny began to scrape off that ribbon. My, how good it tasted!

Suddenly the back door slammed shut with a bang. It startled him so much that he shoved the spoon deep into the pudding. Just then he heard his mother's car in the driveway. Frantically he grabbed the cat and stuck its face and paws in the pudding so that it would be obvious who the culprit was. Then he quickly slipped out to the backyard.

It was not long before Johnny heard his mother call. In the house, the cat was sitting on the couch trying to clean pudding off its face and paws. "Johnny, what kind of foolishness is this?" said Mother. "You know cats do not eat pudding—especially with a spoon." "Be sure your sin will find you out" (Num. 32:23, NKJV).

Lean Not on Your Own Understanding

My friend Ned joined me on one of my annual canoe trips to the Boundary Waters of northern Minnesota. The Boundary Waters allow overnight camping only at designated sites. I had a detailed map indicating where the approved campsites were. The place I had chosen was marked on the map, but it was not visible from the water. We could not tell if it was available or occupied by other canoers. I was in the back of the canoe and maneuvered it to the narrow shoreline. Ned hopped out and climbed up the small bluff. Just as he disappeared over the bluff, he announced, "This is a good campsite."

Still out of sight, Ned asked if I needed help getting out of the canoe. I was insulted by the question and assured him that I was capable of exiting the canoe by myself. Ned kept pestering me, offering to help me get onto the shore. I emphatically repeated that I did not need his help.

Carefully, I put my foot on a rock near the canoe. I put my other foot over the side on another rock and stood up. I did not need any help! The rock I had stepped on shifted, and I instinctively reached for the canoe to steady myself, and the canoe also shifted in the water. Just as Ned came over the bluff, I lost my balance and fell into the lake. We both had a good laugh about it as Ned gave me a hand to get me onto dry land. I should have ignored my pride and accepted his offer of help rather than leaning on the unstable canoe for support. "Trust in the Lord with all your heart; and lean not on your own understanding" (Prov. 3:5, NKJV).

Just Wanted to Get Your Attention

It was the twenty-fifth reunion of the students who graduated at the end of my first year as a boarding school principal. I was eager to meet them after all those years. Some of them I recognized right away. With others, I had to ask for their names. I was approached by four middle-aged women, three of whom I did not recognize. The one I was able to identify asked me if I remembered any special events involving her. I assured her that there was one event I would never forget. One night she had taken an overdose of pills. I rushed her to the hospital emergency room and held her still while the doctor forced her to swallow a charcoal solution to counteract the medicine. It was not a pleasant scene!

The other three women finally revealed their identity and asked if I remembered their confrontation with the rules of the school. It was serious enough to result in suspension for a week. One of them, as I remembered it, was suspended on campus rather than being sent home because her single parent mother worked, and there was no supervision for the girl. She was confined to her dormitory room except for her work assignment.

The three women asked me excitedly if I remembered the incident. I did, but I did not remember what rule they had broken that resulted in such severe discipline. I told them I did not remember what they did, but I did not think it was anything too bad. "I just wanted to get your attention," I said. "Well, you did!" one of them exclaimed. "You certainly did!"

I am reminded that sometimes the Lord has to send us experiences that get our attention. "For the LORD disciplines those he loves, and he punishes each one he accepts as his child." (Heb. 12:6, NLT).

He Purposed in His Heart

It has been my observation that decisions with moral implications are more easily made when individuals have developed a clear sense of who they are as moral entities. Such people are guided more by an internal moral code rather than having to process every individual moral issue that confronts them.

I was at the second of the three Adventist boarding schools I attended during my high school years. Somehow, I found myself in a distant city with two of my friends, Jack and Larry. It was late at night, and we were hungry, so we stopped at a supermarket to buy some snacks. The store appeared to be empty except for a lady at the cash register. As we wandered around trying to decide what we wanted to eat, Jack came up beside me and half whispered, "You want some of these? Just take them. You don't have to pay for them." And with that, he shoved a small item of packaged food inside my coat.

It happened so fast that I did not have a chance to think about it. Just as soon as Jack walked away from where I was standing, I put the package back on the shelf. I did not have to ponder what my response to this situation should be. I had decided long before that I was not a thief. I would never steal from others.

I was fortunate in having made that decision. As soon as I paid for the few things I had, a big guy (the night manager) appeared out of nowhere, grabbed me and literally dragged me out of the store. He accused me of shoplifting and roughly searched me, but he could not find any stolen goods. Someone working in the back of the store had witnessed Jack shoving the packaged food into my coat, but he had not seen me put it back on the shelf.

The story of Daniel and his three friends provides a good pattern to follow. "Daniel purposed in his heart that he would not defile himself" (Dan. 1:8, NKJV).

Water, Cool, Clear Water

When my son was fourteen years old, we decided to go on a backpacking trip on Michigan's Shore to Shore Trail that crosses the Lower Peninsula of the state. There are primitive campgrounds every 20 miles or so along the trail. Some, but not all, have well water available. Our second day of hiking was quite warm and humid. We had exhausted all the water in our canteens long before we got to our destination.

When we arrived at the campsite, there was no well in sight. I was so thirsty my mouth was like cotton. I just had to have something to drink. We boiled water from a little stream to sterilize it. In the process of boiling over the open fire, accumulated debris had gotten into our water. I was so thirsty I just had to drink it anyway. It tasted awful. We pitched our tent and crawled in for the night, still with a terrible thirst.

The next morning, we started up the trail again. My son was ahead of me and disappeared into a little grove of trees out of my sight. Suddenly, he shouted "Oh, no!" I rushed to see what the problem was. There, in the middle of the grove was a well with good, cool, clear water. We had camped within a short distance from good, cool, clear, water, yet we had been drinking warm boiled water with all the debris in it. In this life, we can choose to drink the pure water from Jesus, or we can settle for the debris-filled potion offered by the world. As the scripture states, "They have forsaken me, the spring of living water, and have dug their own cisterns, broken cisterns that cannot hold water" (Jer. 2:13, NIV).

Put on the Whole Armor

On a camping trip in the Boundary Waters Canoe Area Wilderness in northern Minnesota, my friend Jim and I planned to canoe up the eastern arm of Lac La Croix, a large, irregularly shaped lake that formed part of the border with Canada. After spending a couple of days camped on a little island near the border, we made our way down the western arm of the lake and eventually emerged from the Boundary Waters about eight miles from the place where we had parked our vehicle. I volunteered to get the car while Jim hauled our gear up to the parking lot. About half way to my destination I saw a large black object right in the middle of the road about 200 yards ahead of me. I quickly recognized it as a black bear.

I was in no condition to be confronting a bear or any other wild animal. I had been in such a hurry to get on my way that I had neglected to keep my very stout walking stick with me. So I had no weapon to do battle with any creature of the Northwoods. I thought about checking the map to see if there was an alternate route. I quickly discovered that I had left my map back with the rest of our camping gear.

I knew that bears are very nearsighted, so it could not see me very well, though they have a keen sense of smell. I was wearing a hooded sweatshirt that had accumulated quite a bit of debris, including various particles of food. The bear could certainly smell me as I drew nearer to him. I sent a quick prayer to heaven and then started yelling at the bear. He seemed agitated and eventually got up and walked off into the woods. I gave my thanks to the Lord for his protection and hurried on my way. But I determined that, next time, I would not go off on a journey without preparing for such an event.

In the life of the Christian that is good practice. "Put on the whole armor of God, that you may be able to stand against the wiles of the devil" (Eph. 6:11, NKJV).

Part V

The Blessed Hope

A Drink of Cold Water

Joe was ten years old and lived in West Central Minnesota. The event in his life that we will consider took place 100 years ago before small towns had many of the modern conveniences such as electricity and running water. Joe's family got their water from a community well about three blocks from their house. The well pump had a long handle on it and required a good bit of effort to pump a bucketful of water.

The only way to get a good drink of water was to walk the three blocks to the community pump and carry the bucket of water back home so members of the family had something cold to drink. Joe was assigned the job of making sure the bucket always had a sufficient amount of water for the family.

It was a rather cool autumn night when Joe discovered that the bucket of drinking water was almost empty. His father worked on the Great Northern Railroad and was periodically gone for two or three days at a time. Joe knew that, if his father came home and

> *Joe knew that, if his father came home and found the water bucket in that condition, he would be in serious trouble. However, his father had left two days before on his railroad job, and Joe calculated that it would be at least another day before he returned.*

found the water bucket in that condition, he would be in serious trouble. However, his father had left two days before on his railroad job, and Joe calculated that it would be at least another day before he returned. He thought he could get up early enough in the morning to fill a bucketful of water for the rest of the family. Joe went to bed without a worry.

Right in the middle of pleasant dreams, Joe was rudely awakened by his father, who had returned a day earlier than expected. It was not a long conversation. "I want a drink of cold water. The bucket is empty. Go get it filled!" So, Joe had to walk three blocks on that cold, dark night to the community well and carry the bucket of water back home.

Jesus had some instructive words as He spoke to the disciples about His return to earth. "So you also must be ready, because the Son of Man will come at an hour when you do not expect him" (Matt. 24:44, NIV).

"We Have This Hope"—Part One

Several years ago, I toured places of importance in Adventist history. William Miller's home was of special interest. Miller's role in the origins of our denomination is a fascinating study. I slipped away from the group and went out behind the little church beside Miller's home to nearby "Ascension Rock" where it is thought that a group of early Adventists gathered at the time of the "great disappointment." It brought back memories of my own disappointment. Jesus did not come as expected in 1844. Nineteen years later, the Seventh-day Adventist Church was officially founded. Now, a century and a half after its founding, the Seventh-day Adventist Church still awaits Jesus' return.

In 1948 the nation of Israel proclaimed its independence and immediately engaged Arab military forces in battle. Many Adventists thought the battle of Armageddon would take place in the village of Megiddo, located on the edge of the Jezreel Valley (see Rev. 16:16). It would be the last great conflict before the second coming.

I remember hearing older Adventists talking about the seriousness of the times. "We will never see 1950," they proclaimed with great anticipation. However, before the armies could reach Megiddo, a truce was called, and the great battle did not occur. Jesus did not return as we thought He would. My disappointment planted a seed of doubt in my young mind. I could only be sustained by hope. The Adventist hymn can bring comfort. It says: "We have this hope that burns within our hearts, hope in the coming of the Lord." Scripture says, "We have this hope as an anchor for the soul, firm and secure" (Heb. 6:19, NIV).

"We Have This Hope"—Part Two

When I was a boy, a large percentage of Adventists believed that the battle of Armageddon, mentioned in Revelation 16, would be a physical battle involving military forces from the nations of the world. The Arab-Israeli War of 1948 seemed to fit the prophecy. Yet, Jesus did not come, and many of us began to doubt that He ever would come in our lifetime.

Since then, other international events have had potential for erupting into Armageddon. Yet, Jesus never came. Doubt overwhelmed my heart. Then, one day, I happened upon the text in 2 Peter 3 that predicted that scoffers would arise, denying the promise of Jesus' second coming. I realized that the verse was directed right at me.

Other texts jolted me out of my doubt. Hebrews 10:36, 37 admonishes us to have patience for yet a little while. Then, in 2 Peter 3:8, 9, we are reminded that God's time is not our time. With God one day is as a thousand years, so, in reality, Jesus has been gone only a couple of days. Why are we so impatient, I wondered? I should let God run things on His own time schedule, not on mine. Then hope restored my faith. A line from an Adventist hymn provides a solid foundation. "We have this faith that Christ alone imparts, faith in the promise of His word."

"For you have need of endurance, so that after you have done the will of God, you may receive the promise: for yet a little while, *and* He who is coming will come and will not tarry" (Heb. 10:36, 37, NKJV).

Oh, the Dumb Dog!

When I was about ten years old, a retired sheep rancher in southern Wyoming gave us a small dog—a poodle—for a pet. He soon became an integral part of our family although I claimed him as my own. I named him "Teddy." He traveled with us wherever we went.

One time we were on a trip and stopped at a little town to fill our gas tank and stretch our legs a bit. Teddy hopped out of the car with us. After the gas tank was filled, we climbed back into the car and continued our trip. About twenty-five miles down the road, my younger brother, Bob, suddenly discovered something was missing. He let out a yell, "Oh, the dumb dog!" We had failed to get the dog back in the car when we resumed our journey.

We had a short but very intense family council. By unanimous vote, we decided that we couldn't leave Teddy off in a strange place. So we drove the twenty-five miles back to see if he was still there. Sure enough, we found him sitting by the curb, looking expectantly as each car drove by.

When Teddy finally saw the family car, he let out a joyous yelp and quickly clambered into the car when I opened the door. He had waited for a full hour looking for that familiar automobile. He never gave up hope that his family would return to get him. Much like Teddy—"We have this hope that dwells within our heart, hope in the coming of the Lord."

In thinking about Teddy, I'm reminded of the scripture that says, "Looking for the blessed hope and glorious appearing of our great God and Savior Jesus Christ" (Titus 2:13, NKJV).

Quite the Surprise

My friend Jim and I were on a week-long canoe trip in the Boundary Waters Canoe Area Wilderness in northern Minnesota. This is a vast area of lakes and streams that has been set aside for those traveling by non-motorized means. Our planned itinerary took us to Lac La Croix, which is a very large lake that forms part of the border with Canada. The first night we stopped at a marked campsite on a little unnamed island in the big lake. It was getting late in the day, so I gathered up some wood for a fire, and Jim proceeded to cook our supper even before we set up our campsite. While waiting for the food to be cooked, I heard the sound of a crow calling in the distance.

When I mentioned to Jim that the crow seemed especially agitated, he told me that crows are guardians of the forest. Whenever a creature that might be a danger to the more vulnerable inhabitants invades the territory, crows make a big ruckus as a warning. The crow is essentially a lookout for the other creatures, sounding the alarm, "Something is coming through the forest! Something is coming through the forest!"

> *The crow is essentially a lookout for the other creatures, sounding the alarm, "Something is coming through the forest! Something is coming through the forest!"*

Twenty minutes later, I heard a rustling at the edge of our campsite. I looked up to see a big black bear lumbering out of the woods. That was quite the surprise! The bear didn't seem intimidated by our presence. When he got a whiff of the food we were cooking, he developed a real interest in our campsite. I was not ready for such an encounter. The bear caught me by surprise, though the warning of the crow should have told me that something was coming through the forest.

The Bible tells us that Somebody is coming through the clouds someday. We do not need to be surprised when that event occurs because we have been warned about the conditions that will precede His coming. The promise of Jesus' second coming was given to His closest disciples as He left this earth. "This same Jesus, who has been taken from you into heaven, will come back in the same way you have seen him go into heaven" (Acts 1:11, NIV).

Time to Wake Up!

Several years ago, I was employed as the principal of a coeducational secondary boarding school. We had over a hundred teenagers living in the two dormitories on campus in addition to twenty-five or thirty students who lived in the village. My wife and I lived in a house right on the school campus. We were responsible for the care and safety of the students twenty-four hours a day.

One night about 11 o'clock the dean in charge of the boy's dormitory called me with an anxious message. One of the boys was missing. His roommate did not recall seeing him at recreation time. A search of the campus did not locate him. I walked quickly to the dormitory, which was about 100 yards from my house. There I met the dean who was very concerned about the missing student. We were standing in the second-floor hallway where the boy's room was. Suddenly we heard a noise down the hall and looked up to see our missing teenager stumbling down the hall, looking as if he had just awakened from a deep sleep.

The teenager told us the story. He had decided to play a trick on a friend that lived at the other end of the hallway. During recreation time he managed to get into the room and hid in the closet. He planned to jump out and scare his friend when he went to bed. It was warm in the closet, and he was tired, so he fell into a sound sleep. He had just now awakened.

As I thought about that experience, I realized that it is very easy for the Christian to fall into a slumber and miss the seriousness of the times in which we live. "The hour has already come for you to wake up from your slumber, because our salvation is nearer now than when we first believed" (Rom. 13:11, NIV).

The Heavens Declare

I was exhausted when we finally reached our destination, a campsite on the south shore of Knife Lake, a long narrow body of water that forms part of the border with Canada. My friend Ray and I were on a canoe trip in the Boundary Waters Wilderness in Northern Minnesota. The weather did not look good, so we quickly got our camp set up and prepared a rather primitive evening meal. By sunset, it had begun to rain a little, though not hard. It was just enough to make it a miserable experience. I had taken an annual canoe trip for several years, so I was hardly a novice. What surprised me on this trip were the long, steep portages we had to carry our canoe between the different waterways.

The call of the loons made for pleasant background music. Ray, who had gone for a walk, suddenly called me. "Jerry, come quick. You need to see this!" I ran down to the lake shore and saw the most amazing sight imaginable. The whole northern sky was lit up with what looked like giant spotlights on the Canadian side of the lake. The lights displayed a variety of soft pastel colors. It was the most exotic display of the aurora borealis, or Northern Lights, I had ever seen.

I sat there transfixed for more than an hour. My mind immediately went to Psalm 19. "The heavens declare the glory of God; the skies proclaim the work of his hands" (Ps. 19:1, NIV). There I was—right in the midst of God's handiwork. What an opportunity to commune with my Maker! Later, as I reminisced about the experience, I thought of another promise about the future. "Eye has not seen, nor ear heard, nor have entered into the heart of man the things which God has prepared for those who love Him" (1 Cor. 2, 9, NKJV).

Part VI

Other Observations

I Do Not Know Why I Stopped

Clark was a pipefitter in the roundhouse on the Union Pacific Railroad in southern Wyoming. It was a good job and paid well. His work required that he be on call even on his days off, as well as on holidays. Clark was not a particularly religious person. His only contact with a church had been in his early childhood when his grandmother took him to the Seventh-day Adventist church where they lived. Eventually his family moved away, but the memories of his grandmother and her faith were the only thing he knew about God and the Bible.

The new Adventist minister in town had somehow gotten his name as possibly being interested in further study of his grandmother's religion. Clark arranged to have the minister come to his house one evening each week for formal Bible studies. The entire family enjoyed these sessions, and soon they were in regular attendance at Sabbath services. That is, except for Clark, who continued to be assigned work on Saturdays even though he had asked to have that day off. This caused him a great deal of mental anguish. He wanted to keep the Sabbath, yet he also wanted to keep his job.

One Friday evening, Clark didn't finish his work assignment until an hour after sundown. Hurriedly, he started across the rail

> *Just a few seconds later he felt something tugging at his side and looked up to see the big iron wheels of the yard engine against his body.*

yard, but tripped and fell across the track. Just a few seconds later he felt something tugging at his side and looked up to see the big iron wheels of the yard engine against his body. As he struggled to get up, the driver of the yard engine appeared by his side and helped him get up on his feet. "I don't know why I stopped the engine where I did," he said in a serious voice. "Something just seemed to tell me to stop." As Clark reflected on his near brush with tragedy, he got a new look at the meaning of life and decided that keeping the Sabbath holy was more important than keeping the good job he had.

I was privileged to witness Clark and his entire family baptized in the natural hot springs pool in Saratoga, Wyoming. A precious promise is found in the Scripture. "Though I walk in the midst of trouble, You will revive me; You will stretch out Your hand against the wrath of my enemy and Your right hand will save me" (Ps. 138:7, NKJV).

Why are You Looking at that Field?

It was my first year as a boarding school principal. I was well prepared academically for the job and had sufficient administrative experience. What I was not prepared for was farming. This school had 200 acres of farmland in which they grew corn and soybeans. Suddenly, the market section of the newspaper became a very important part of my life.

That was a challenge in my first year as principal. With a wet fall and an early snow, the farm manager was unable to get his machinery out in the fields to harvest the soybeans. I calculated that, with the normal yield and the current price, the crop should provide about $25,000. That was potentially a big loss. Winter came early that year, and the field was covered with a blanket of snow. Those in the know told me that there was little hope of harvesting the soybeans when springtime came and the snow melted.

I was almost to the point of despondency regarding the financial loss that we were about to incur. One day I was sitting at my desk in the office looking out the big picture window at the field of soybeans buried under the snow when a local farmer walked into my office. "Why are you looking out at that field?" he asked. "Those soybeans do not belong to you! This school is doing God's work, and that field belongs to Him. Let Him worry about it."

That was just the message I needed to hear. I took his advice and trusted the Lord to take care of *His* field of soybeans. When spring came, the beans were still off the ground and in good condition. We got a good yield that helped us meet our financial needs. "The earth *is* the LORD's and the fulness thereof; the world, and they that dwell therein" (Ps. 24:1).

I Can Sure Tell That You Are Brothers

"I can sure tell that you and Joe are brothers. The resemblance is so strong," said a recent acquaintance of mine. I had recently moved to the state where my youngest brother had lived for several years. Joe is nineteen years younger than I am, so we really did not grow up in the same home. In fact, I had the distinct impression that my parents did not enforce the same rigid set of rules on him that they had used on me. They had mellowed a lot by the time he came along.

Even though we never lived together at home, we had several things in common. We both arrived in this world under unusual conditions. When I was born, my birth mother gave me away at three days of age. I was taken by a lady and transported to West Central Minnesota where I was taken in by a tenant farmer. Eleven months later my new mother passed away, and I was once again a motherless child. My new father married his deceased wife's sister, and she was the one I knew as Mom. Nineteen years later, Mom and a friend drove into the parking lot of a small hospital in the northern part of Michigan's Lower Peninsula. A lady came out of the hospital carrying a newborn baby and handed it through the window of the car to Mom. That's how Joe became my brother. Eventually our adoptive parents got legal custody of him so that he had proper documentation. For me, I was nearly sixty years old before I got a valid birth certificate.

Even though we don't carry the same genetic code and we grew up under different circumstances, my youngest brother, Joe, and I are the closest of friends. Somehow our mannerisms and our interests are so similar that people have no trouble thinking that we are blood brothers. We have the same faith in God and His leading in our lives. My new acquaintance was very surprised when I told him that Joe and I were not at all related.

> Even though we don't carry the same genetic code and we grew up under different circumstances, my youngest brother, Joe, and I are the closest of friends.

The Scripture says, "How wonderful it is when brothers live together in peace and harmony" (Ps. 133:1, my paraphrase). It also points to our membership in the family of God. "God decided in advance to adopt us into his own family by bringing us to himself through Jesus Christ" (Eph. 1:5, NLT).

Earthy Words

Several years ago, I was a member of a political club and was involved in a number of its activities. I was the only Seventh-day Adventist in the group and frequently faced conflicts with activities that I wanted to attend because they were scheduled on Friday night or Sabbath. I made it very clear to the other members that from sundown Friday to sundown Saturday was sacred time to me and that I should not be expected to attend meetings or engage in other political activities during that time each week.

Until that time in my life, most of my social acquaintances were members of my own Seventh-day Adventist faith community. This was my first real immersion into a strictly secular organization. There might have been others in the club who were practicing Christians, but it was not apparent. I did not make a big deal about my spiritual inclinations, I just tried to live my faith.

One of the club's activities was to have a booth at the county fair every August. We pitched a large tent that people could visit to rest, talk politics, or purchase political paraphernalia we had for sale. It took a lot of preparation to get ready for fair week, and I tried to help as much as possible. One day, another club member and I were putting the finishing touches on our large tent. I was adjusting the rope that was tied to an upright pole when my hands slipped and got caught between the pole and the rope. As the pole shifted, the rope tightened around my hand, and I experienced a sudden sharp pain. I let fly a slang term that substituted for an expletive. It was not actual profanity or swearing but just a word of exclamation.

My friend looked at me in puzzlement. "Jerry," he said, "those are the first earthy words I have ever heard you say!" I was surprised by the comment. I did not know that my behavior was so markedly different that anyone would notice how I talked or the language I used. I determined that he would never hear "earthy words" from my mouth again. "Let no corrupt word proceed out of your mouth, but what is good for necessary edification, that it may impart grace to the hearers" (Eph. 4:29, NKJV).

A Father's Counsel to a Wayward Son

As a teenager, I did a lot of foolish things—none of which I will describe in detail. However, I did have some experiences that made a lasting impression on me. It happened at the second of the three boarding schools that I was privileged to attend. I had a tendency to view all the rules of the school as being overly restrictive because they were imposed arbitrarily by the adults. I began to think of requirements in the student handbook more as suggestions for me to consider than as rules requiring strict adherence.

Eventually, along with a bad attitude, I far overstepped the bounds of acceptable behavior. In response, the faculty voted that the school would be a better place if I were not among the student body. Suddenly, I liked the school. All my griping and complaining about how bad it was there seemed to fade away. I wanted to stay there more than anything else.

I called my father who listened to my complaint about how the school had mistreated me, though I still wanted to stay there. Then Dad gave me some advice about how to approach the situation. I remember the tone if not the exact words. "Son," he said, "let me make a suggestion. Get down on your hands and knees, crawl down the hallway to the principal's office, grab him around the ankles and beg him with all your heart to stay at the school. Cry and blubber and make all kinds of promises to obey the rules. If the faculty is foolish enough to let you stay, I will let you finish the year there. Otherwise, pack your suitcase and come home so I can keep track of you."

I took Dad's counsel and approached the administration with much humility. The faculty was convened once again, and they voted that I could stay there, but I would be under a very restrictive set of rules. I managed to finish the year without further drama. Dad's counsel helped me improve my attitude towards authority and rules of order. That memory has guided me for 65 years. "Listen, my son, accept what I say, and the years of your life will be many" (Prov. 4:10, NIV).

You Have to Decide

One day, in my second year of college, several of my friends gathered in my dormitory room. We were laughing and joking like guys can do. One friend, whom I will call Wendell, was sitting on the top bunk, and, as I noticed him getting ready to jump off the bed, a mischievous thought came into my mind. While he was still airborne, I gave him a slight shove which threw him off balance. He landed on the floor with arms and legs flying every which direction. Instantly, he started cursing at me. He had a tremendous command of swear words, which spewed out with a great deal of volume and emotion. Immediately, one of my other friends (I will call him Lawrence) found the language the Wendell was using very offensive and, without saying a word, immediately left the room.

> You have two sets of friends, your righteous friends and your wicked friends. You have to decide which group you are going to be with."

I was embarrassed and angry with Wendell. "You know better than to use language like that when Lawrence is here," I said. Wendell struggled to his feet, pointed his finger right in my chest, and said, "That is the trouble with you, Jerry. You have two sets of friends, your righteous friends and your wicked friends. You have to decide which group you are going to be with."

That caught me by surprise. I had never thought I would have to make such a hard choice. I liked both sets of friends, and I agonized over the decision for several weeks. One Friday night, I was alone in my dormitory room. With my indecisiveness weighing heavy on my mind, I perceived that I could delay no longer. Right then I said to God, "I am with you!" I still had my two sets of friends, but I found myself gradually losing interest in things that captivated my wicked friends. Several years previously I had been born of the water. I was now born of the Spirit.

When Nicodemus came to Jesus by night to learn the way of salvation, Jesus said, "Except a man be born of water and of the Spirit, he cannot enter into the kingdom of God" (John 3:5).

When the Answer Is "No"

I believe in the power of prayer. Yet, I am aware of the experience of the Apostle Paul, who prayed three times for relief from a debilitating physical condition. The response from God was, "My grace is sufficient for thee." In other words, "I will help you deal with it."

One summer, our three great-granddaughters came to visit along with their parents and grandparents. Our family tradition at mealtime is to hold hands around the table and ask God's blessing on the food. One day, as we gathered for our meal, I noticed the four-year-old protesting to her mother about the food already placed on her plate. When she settled down, her seven-year-old sister said the prayer. The moment "Amen" was pronounced, the younger child asked me, "Grandpa, can I pray?" Here is what she prayed: "Dear God," she started with great sincerity, "I do not like this food! I did not ask for this food! I do not want this food! Amen."

We stifled our laughs, not wanting to mock her sincerity. Her mother overruled her appeal to a Higher Power, and she had to eat the food that was set before her.

We should not let a "no" answer to prayer be a challenge to our faith in God's promise that He will answer prayer. On the night before the crucifixion, Jesus prayed that he might be spared the terrible events awaiting Him. He completed his plea, "Father, if thou be willing, remove this cup from me: nevertheless, not my will, but thine, be done" (Luke 22:42). This is the pattern for all believers as we claim the promises of God regarding answers to our prayers.

Why the Baby Cried

I was sound asleep, but I was having a major nightmare. It was the end of the semester at the second Adventist boarding school I attended during my high school years. That meant major exams tomorrow, and I was not quite prepared—even though I had engaged in intense study (that is, cramming) for two days. In my frightful dream, I could see the exam questions and realized I would be labeled a failure for the rest of my life.

While I was having this nightmare, about 300 yards from our dormitory, the infant son of Mr. Baker, the Bible teacher, was also having a bad night. The baby was usually a sound sleeper but not this night. Shortly after midnight the baby abruptly awoke from whatever mental image was tormenting him, and he let out a piercing wail that instantly woke his parents. Mr. Baker bounded out of bed and rushed to his young offspring. On a quick look out the window, he noticed flames coming from the basement of the music building that was located between the two dormitories.

The boiler that heated the entire campus was in the basement of that building. Evidently an electrical circuit failed and started a fire. He quickly put on his shoes and grabbed his heavy overcoat. As Mr. Baker raced out the door he shouted to his wife. "Call the boy's dean. I will wake up the boys."

I was awakened from my nightmare by the sound of the Bible teacher pounding on the doors as he ran down the hall shouting "Boys, boys, wake up." My room was on the side toward the music building, and I immediately saw the flames leaping from the basement. It was not long before the wind whipped the flames towards the dormitory and it, being a wood structure, burned to the ground. Fortunately, because we had an early warning, none of the students suffered injury from the fire.

As I think about this experience, I am reminded of the words in Psalm 91: "Thou shalt not be afraid for the terror by night" (Ps. 91:5). And that's why the baby cried.

Which the Wind Drives Away

When I was 16 years of age, I got a job working as a farm hand in Wyoming's Bighorn Basin, where we lived at the time. I was proud to have a man's job and to earn a man's wage. The going rate for fieldwork at that time was five dollars a day plus room and board. I forgot to ask what the definition of a "day" was before I took the job. We rose from our sleep before daylight and, after chores, went to the farmhouse for breakfast. We worked in the fields until about one o'clock, at which time we returned to the farmhouse for dinner, which was prepared by the farmer's wife. After a short nap, the farmer took us back to the field where we worked until nearly dark.

I was 16 years old and was being paid a man's wage so I thought I should have a tractor-driving job. Much to my surprise, the farmer's eight-year-old daughter drove the tractor, with a trailer behind it, through the fields where the sheaves (bundles) of grain had been stacked upright in shocks. My job was to walk beside the trailer and pitch the bundles onto it. When the trailer was full, we drove to the threshing machine where we pitched the bundles onto the conveyor belt. The machine did the work of separating the grain from the stem of the plant. The remaining debris, known as chaff, was blown out the back end of the thrasher. By noon there was a billowing cloud of chaff being driven hither and yon by the never-ceasing Wyoming winds.

The righteous are like trees rooted and grounded in Jesus. They stand in stark contrast to the wicked who "*are* like chaff which the wind drives away" (Psalm 1:4, NKJV).

Seeking Whom He May Devour

For several years I took a week off each summer for a camping trip in the Boundary Waters Canoe Area Wilderness in northern Minnesota. On one memorable trip, my friend Jim joined me. We parked our vehicle in a designated area and started out with a half-mile portage to Moose River. Our plan was to canoe up to Lac La Croix, a large irregularly shaped lake that formed part of the border with Canada.

After spending a couple days there, we made our way down the western arm of the lake and emerged from the Boundary Waters, about eight miles from the place we had parked our vehicle. I volunteered to get the car while Jim hauled all of our gear from the river up to the parking area. It took me about three hours to walk to the place where we had left our vehicle. I quickly jumped in and drove the eight miles back to where Jim was. As I drove into the area where several cars and trucks were parked, I noticed Jim was standing on top of a station wagon. I called out, "Jim, what are you doing up there?"

He told me that, as soon as he had gotten all our gear hauled up from the river landing, he was confronted by a black bear. Jim gathered up several stones that were in good supply and managed to drive the bear away from our gear. Yet, then the bear began to approach him in a menacing manner. That is why he had climbed on top of the station wagon. He had been in that spot of safety for nearly two hours. Not seeing any evidence of the bear's presence, we quickly stowed our possessions in the car, affixed the canoe on top, and left the site before the bear appeared again.

In thinking about Jim's confrontation with the bear, I was reminded of a Bible verse: "Be sober, be vigilant; because your adversary the devil walks about like a roaring lion, seeking whom he may devour" (1 Peter 5:8, NKJV).

Her Firstborn Son

My birth mother gave me up for adoption three days after I was born, and I was taken in by a tenant farmer in central Minnesota. However, my new mother was quite ill, and she died eleven months later. My adopted father married his first wife's younger sister, and she is the one I grew up knowing as Mom. I didn't know for several years after she passed away that it had not been her choice to adopt me but that she got stuck taking care of me because her older sister had sickened and died. In all the years I lived with Mom, she never indicated anything other than that I was her firstborn son and that I carried a special place in her heart. I never had an inkling that I was not her chosen child.

In her later years, Mom succumbed to the ravages of cancer. My wife is stronger emotionally than I am, and she is the one who went to see the specialist with Mom and to receive the news that Mom had about six weeks left to live. That left her with the task of telling Mom about her limited future and conveying that message to the rest of the family. I have a vivid memory of Mom's last words to me. "Oh, Jerry, I need to tell you …" And, with that, she lost her ability to speak and never was able to finish her sentence. To this day I don't know what it was that she was trying to tell me.

In thinking about the events of my life, I have become much more aware of the shortness of human time on this earth. How I wish I had been able to convey to my mother the love I had for her as I became aware of the situation when she took me in as her own. My memory of Mom is a pattern of the gift of our Heavenly Father as we are blessed with adoption into the family of God.

"The Spirit Himself bears witness with our spirit that we are the children of God, and if children, then heirs—heirs of God, and joint heirs with Christ" (Rom. 8:16, 17, NKJV).

Mom.

Jerry and Reva Furst.

TEACH Services, Inc.
P U B L I S H I N G
www.TEACHServices.com • (800) 367-1844

We invite you to view the complete
selection of titles we publish at:
www.TEACHServices.com

We encourage you to write us
with your thoughts about this,
or any other book we publish at:
info@TEACHServices.com

TEACH Services' titles may be purchased in
bulk quantities for educational, fund-raising,
business, or promotional use.
bulksales@TEACHServices.com

Finally, if you are interested in seeing
your own book in print, please contact us at:
publishing@TEACHServices.com
We are happy to review your manuscript at no charge.